ABSTRACT

AFRICAN AMERICAN STUDIES

SULLIVAN, NICOLE L.   B.A. TROY UNIVERSITY, 2010

<u>MENTORING AND EDUCATIONAL OUTCOMES OF BLACK GRADUATE STUDENTS</u>

Committee Chair: James Young, Ph.D.

Thesis dated May 2015

The purpose of this research is to examine the ways in which mentoring affects black graduate students' completion of programs of study. Performance is measured by completion of their graduate program, length of time taken to complete the program, grade point average (GPA), and overall attitude about their graduate school experience. On average, over half of all black graduate students leave their programs of study before completion compared to 25% attrition (non-completion of program of study) of white students.

A review of the literature suggests that any form of mentoring improves completion rates among black graduate students. Existing research further suggests that when paired with like mentors, such as same race or gender, black graduate students complete their programs at even higher rates. The existing research is, however, limited due to the age of the research and factors such as attrition by discipline. Updated research is needed to determine why, despite being admitted to graduate programs of study at the highest rates in United States history, black students are leaving without graduate degrees more than any other race.

Vincent Tinto's theory of social adjustment states that students who are not socially adjusted are less likely to persist (complete their program of study). Because black students are attending Predominately White Institutions (PWI's) at the highest rates since Reconstruction, this research will examine ways in which black graduate students become socially adjusted and how it affects their persistence.

The anticipated results of the study are that black graduate students who had mentors completed their programs more often than those who did not have mentors. Additionally, those who had mentors of the same race, gender, or socio-economic backgrounds may report even higher percentages of completion. In contrast, those who did not have mentors may report lower percentages of completion.

MENTORING AND EDUCATIONAL OUTCOMES OF BLACK GRADUATE

STUDENTS

A THESIS

SUBMITTED TO THE FACULTY OF CLARK ATLANTA UNIVERSITY

IN PARTIAL FULFILLMENT OF THE REQUIREMENTS FOR

THE DEGREE OF MASTER OF ARTS

BY

NICOLE SULLIVAN

DEPARTMENT OF AFRICAN AMERICAN STUDIES, AFRICANA WOMEN'S

STUDIES, AND HISTORY

ATLANTA, GEORGIA

MAY 2015

STATEMENT OF UNDERSTANDING

Clark Atlanta University Theses or Dissertations
Deposited in the Robert W. Woodruff Library of the Atlanta University Center, Inc.

Document Submitted: Thesis X____   Dissertation _____

Document Title:
<u>MENTORING AND EDUCATIONAL OUTCOMES OF BLACK GRADUATE</u>
<u>STUDENTS</u>

Robert W. Woodruff Library of the Atlanta University Center, Inc. is organized
exclusively to operate an academic library for the benefit of Clark Atlanta University,
The Interdenominational Theological Center, Morehouse College, and Spelman
College. As such, the Library is granted the non-exclusive right to archive, reproduce,
and distribute my thesis or dissertation in whole or in part in all formats, available now
or in future. I acknowledge and grant permission for distribution and use of my thesis
or dissertation for scholarly and research purposes only. Distribution and use of my
thesis or dissertation in whole or in part for commercial purposes requires my written
permission.

I understand that I retain ownership of copyright of the thesis or dissertation. I also
retain the right to use in future works (such as articles or books) all or part of this thesis
or dissertation. I have obtained and attached, as appropriate, written permission
statement(s) from the owner(s) of each third party copyrighted matter to be included in
my thesis or dissertation, allowing distribution and use as specified above. I agree that
permission to quote from, to copy from, or to publish this thesis/dissertation may be
granted by the author or, in his/her absence, the Dean of the School of The College of
Arts and Sciences at Clark Atlanta University.

I certify that the version submitted is the same as that officially approved by my thesis or
dissertation committee and Department Chair and submitted to the offices of the Dean of
the School and Graduate Studies.

_____   _____
Signature of Author   Date

TABLE OF CONTENTS

CHAPTER 1: INTRODUCTION

Purpose and Rationale

"In academia, mentored. . .students have been found to have a higher GPA, more units completed per semester, and a lower dropout rate than their non-mentored counterparts."[1] The purpose of this statement and thesis is to explore mentor relationships to determine what factors impact black students' completion of graduate programs of study. This research will examine the ways in which mentoring impacts black graduate students' decision to complete their programs of study and what factors ultimately cause some to leave their programs of study without completing. Factors to be considered are the need for black faculty, social adjustment, and the availability of mentors. On average, over half of all black graduate students leave their programs of study without completing, compared to just 25% of other races.[2]

This thesis will consider Vincent Tinto's Theory of Social Adjustment to determine in what ways social adjustment, or lack thereof, affects attrition among black graduate students. Tinto's theory posits that students who are not socially adjusted tend to leave their programs of study without completion. With black students attending Predominately White Institutions (PWI's) in the highest numbers since Reconstruction

---

[1] Laura L. Paglis and Stephen G. Green and Talya N. Bauert, "Does Adviser Mentoring Add Value? A Longitudinal Study of Mentoring and Doctoral Student Outcomes, " *Research in Higher Education* 47, No. 4 (2006): 452.
[2] Ibid.

and the average number of black faculty at PWI's is less than 4%, it is possible that students may struggle to become socially adjusted in a sea of white faces. This thesis will attempt to determine the social factors that lead to successful outcomes of black graduate students and what factors motivate them to persist in their programs of study. For the purpose of this thesis, mentoring relationships can be formal or informal. Moberg and Velasquez define mentoring as a means of handing down tradition, supporting talent, and securing future leadership.[3]

Mentors are often faculty members who understand the needs of students. They impart wisdom, discipline, and structure. Mentors can often warn students of potential pitfalls that await them in higher education. In more formal mentoring programs, mentors prepare letters of recommendation, provide information on scholarships, and leads on employment opportunities. In order for mentors to be able to offer such a wide array of services, they must first get to know the student, empathize, and be able to relate. Therefore, mentors and their mentees must share things in common. A mentee may select or be assigned a mentor based on a number of factors, such as program of study, specific interests, age, gender, and ethnicity. Mentees who have a variety of interests or are enrolled in a popular program of study are easy to pair with a mentor. However, attempting to pair minority mentees based on ethnicity can become cumbersome, if not problematic. With more black students attending Predominately White Institutions (PWI's) than ever before, and fewer than 4% of faculty at most PWI's being black, most

---

[3] Dennis J. Moberg and Manuel Velasquez, "The Ethics of Mentoring," *Business Ethics Quarterly* 14, No. 1 (2004): 95.

of those black students will be mentored by white faculty. In many cases, they may receive no mentoring at all.

Studies, such as the NCSU 1992 study and the UTP study,[4] show that black graduate students with same-race mentors tend to perform better, than those with white mentors, and have better educational outcomes. Performance is measured in terms of grades, whether they completed the program, and length of time taken to complete the program. Quality of educational outcomes is measured in terms of readiness to assimilate into the academy and overall attitude of their experience. While some report that having a same-race mentor improved their overall graduate experience, others cite simply having a mentor as a factor that contributed to their contentment with their experience. Still, others who reported having no mentor at all reported completing their program of study in an acceptable time, with good grades, and an overall good experience. However, research supports the notion that mentoring is critical to positive educational outcomes, including completion. Much of the available research advocates mentoring relationships for graduate success.

Many experts agree that same-race mentoring among blacks leads to more academic success. While not all agree that same-race mentoring is crucial to success, they agree that nurturing relationships between people of similar experiences, backgrounds, etc., lead to better overall performance among graduate students. ". . .a lack of familiarity

---

[4] Wynetta Y. Lee, "Striving Toward Effective Retention: The Effect of Race on Mentoring African American Students," *Peabody Journal of Education* 74, no. 2, Mentoring Underrepresented Students in Higher Education (1999): 27-43.

with the background and expectations of African American students account for infrequent socialization among students."[5]

Statement of the Problem

In 1994, Provost Alison Richards of Yale University fired a shot heard around the academy. She stated that there were no more than 120 qualified black PhDs to serve as university professors and she was not about to enter into a bidding war for their services. However inaccurate her statement, it would become known as the Pipeline Defense: Universities are not diversified in their hiring of black faculty because there are not any to hire. While some fired back and found Dr. Richard's statement inflammatory and untrue, let us assume for a moment that she is correct. What we know for a fact is that Predominantly White Institutions (PWI's) are admitting more black students than at any other time in history. Therefore, if there are none qualified to teach, then that means Dr. Richards and others are not doing their jobs because they are not retaining the students they admit. They are not graduating PhDs in comparable numbers. What is happening between the time black graduate students are admitted to PhD programs at PWI's and prior to graduation is that they are leaving the programs. Studies show that lack of funding and insufficient grades are not prevailing reasons. By and large, black students are leaving because they are not socially adjusted, they lack adequate mentoring, and there is little, if any presence of black faculty to encourage the student to continue.

---

[5] Anna L. Green and LaKita V. Scott, *Journey to the Ph.D.: How to Navigate the Process as African Americans* (Virginia: Stylus Publishing, 2003), 230.

Although more blacks are attending Predominately White Institutions (PWI's) than in past decades, retention of black students continues to dwindle. Many PWI's choose to view the inability of some black students to complete their programs as failures on the part of the student. However, black students who do not receive adequate mentoring tend to perform poorly in graduate programs and either leave the program, or struggle through and post mediocre grades. Students who enter into nurturing mentoring relationships tend to not only complete their program in an acceptable amount of time, but do so with great academic success. One of the problems is that many PWI's not only lack sufficient number of black faculty compared to the number of black students, but also lack adequate mentoring programs that pair black students with mentors who are genuinely consigned to their success. According to Green and Scott, "Research consistently shows African Americans attending PWI's experience more stress, racism, and isolation, and are less likely to persist than their counterparts."[6]

This paper will explore the need for more black faculty at PWI's and in what ways mentoring relationships can benefit black graduate students. Faculty members are often overworked and underappreciated, viewing the task of mentoring students an additional, thankless burden. However, studies further show that effective mentoring relationships not only benefit the student, but also the mentor. Faculty members who mentor students can find a renewed sense of purpose by seeing what a few words of encouragement can do to catapult a student's academic career. That is not to say that a mentor simply encourages students, as that is only part of the process. "Mentoring has been classically defined as a process by which persons of superior rank, special

---

[6] Ibid., 229.

achievements, and prestige instruct, counsel, guide, and facilitate the intellectual (or career) development of persons identified as protégés or mentees."[7]

It is important to note that not all of the existing literature points to same-race mentoring as a means of preparing black graduate students for the academy. In fact, many PWI's and research universities that have formal mentoring partnership programs in place do not focus on race as a factor when pair mentors with students. Many programs focus on programs of study and interests when matching faculty members with their mentees. Therefore, the research in this thesis will explore multiple mentor-mentee pairings to determine what factors ultimately impact black graduate students' experience as a graduate student, especially at PWI's. The University of Michigan (UMich) is one such example of a research university that focuses heavily on mentoring. UMich, as it is affectionately known, has more than 20 formal mentoring programs in various schools and centers across the university. Additionally, they make available two handbooks on mentoring.

One of the handbooks is for faculty use, which outlines effective ways to mentor graduate students. Another handbook is geared towards graduate students and it has suggestions for finding the right mentor. While it does emphasize compatibility, it does not advocate focusing on race when selecting a mentor. However, unlike many other PWI's and research institutions, UMich does not lack adequate numbers of black faculty. While the national percentage hovers around 4% for black faculty, University of

---

[7] Regina Dixon-Reeves, "Mentoring as a Precursor to Incorporation: An Assessment of the Mentoring Experience of Recently Minted Ph.D.s," *Journal of black Studies* 34, No. 1, Race in the Academy: Moving beyond Diversity and toward the Incorporation of Faculty of Color in Predominantly White Colleges and Universities (2003): 15.

Michigan boasts nearly twice that number.[8] With a black faculty to black student ratio of 1:1, Michigan is one of the most diverse, most progressive research universities in the country. In 2009, University of Michigan awarded 2% of all the PhDs conferred on black students in the country. Considering it is only 0.001% of the PhD-granting institutions in the country,[9] this figure is astounding. While that certainly was not always the case, University of Michigan has made great strides in the last 40 years.

For the purpose of this study, a mentor is a faculty member who enters into a relationship with a student for the purpose of offering guidance and encouragement during their academic career. The mentor is not compensated, except through the benefit of the relationship. In one instance, the student reported having thought that his advisor was actually his mentor because of the encouragement and guidance he received. In some ways, he was correct. The advisor went the extra mile to ensure that the student had the tools needed to succeed. This kind of interaction can be considered an informal mentoring relationship. However, in a structured mentor/mentee relationship, the mentor is expected to meet with the student regularly to ensure that the student is on course towards completion. However, the student is responsible for ensuring that the meetings take place regularly. Missed appointments and cancellations signal problems in either the relationship or with the student. In such a case, intervention is necessary to ensure that the student is making adequate progress and is receiving the support needed to complete the program in a timely manner.

---

[8] U.S. Department of Education, http://www.ed.gov/ (accessed July 26, 2012).
[9] National Center for Education Statistics, http://nces.ed.gov/fastfacts/display.asp?id=72 (accessed July 26, 2012).

At Historically Black Colleges and Universities (HBCU's), great care must be taken to create mentor relationships that are not patronizing and enabling, but are structured and not a substitute for hard work. Mentors at HBCU's must not give a pass to students simply because they are black or because they may have been denied opportunities elsewhere. Mentors must prepare the student for the world by simulating it. Mentors must demand that students contribute meaningfully to the relationship and not just pacify the student by telling him what he wants to hear. To do anything less would be to do an even greater injustice than not providing mentorship at all. black faculty members have an exponentially greater responsibility to the student because they have been in their position and know what black graduates need in a mentor.

When it comes to mentoring at PWI's, the presence of black faculty is as encouraging at the mentoring relationship itself. It signals the student that there is a place for him post-graduation. However, if black faculty members do not reach out to their junior counterparts, their existence may never be known to the students who need them. The mentoring relationships can produce additional benefits when it extends beyond the campus walls. Mentors who provide opportunities for their mentees to socialize outside of the classroom further signal to the student that they are more than a number. When a student feels they are valued beyond their tuition dollars, they are more likely to complete their program and report a positive graduate experience.

The mentoring relationship is a two-way street and it must not be incumbent upon the mentor to either initiate or maintain healthy interaction with the mentee. It is the responsibility of the mentee to communicate his needs. The mentor can only act on knowledge, not assumptions. However, in most cases, mentees are simply seeking encouragement. While ". . .discussing the frustrations and challenges of the doctoral program [at PWI's]," one female had this to say about her same-race mentors: "The intensity of their desire to see me do well has provided me with a sense of fortitude and strength. I feel as though I am standing on the shoulders of my predecessors. I'm able to conquer this mountain because. . .they've paved the way. . .These persons have functions as role models, advisors, mentors, and friends."[10]

A mentor is defined as someone who offers meaningful support, whether formally or informally, that results in positive educational or social outcomes for the student. A student can have more than one mentor, as different mentors may have different support to offer. A mentoring relationship can be as casual as a monthly email to see how things are going or as formal as scheduled weekly face-to-face appointments. The most important factor in a healthy mentor-mentee relationship is that the needs of the mentee are either met or surpassed. Usually, the only outcome the mentor is seeking is feedback based on their advice and encouragement. One student reported nearly a dozen mentors during her graduate career. Each mentor had something unique to offer, something each of the others did not. While one mentor may focus on the academic needs of the student, another may bring emotional or social encouragement when it is sensed that something is amiss. A kind word or gesture may occur at a crucial time when a student is on the cusp of leaving the program and looking for the proverbial sign that they should stay.

---

[10] Green and Scott, *Journey to the Ph.D.: How to Navigate the Process as African Americans*, 207.

Methodology

The proposed methodology for conducting research is to survey members of the National Black Graduate Student Association. This population represents black graduate students from around the United States. A sample from this group can produce reliable results. Students will be asked a range of questions, starting with demographics like what kind of undergraduate institution they attended. They will be asked about their mentoring relationships, both formal and informal. If they left their program, they will be asked about the reasons they left prior to completion. They will also answer questions about their post-program experience. For example, they will answer questions about whether they have found employment in their trained field and how satisfied they are about their overall experience. For those who choose to participate, interviews will be conducted to glean in-depth information about their experience.

Particular interest will be paid to those who discuss the development of mentoring programs based on the perceived need at the time of creation of the programs. Also, there will be particular focus on students who left their program before completion, since one of the primary focuses of this thesis is reasons for black attrition. Data will be collected and coded to ensure the integrity of the data collected. Findings will be reported in the Results chapter of the thesis. The results will be analyzed to determine if research questions were answered and if the thesis statement was supported by findings.

Research Questions

1. In what ways does mentoring affect performance and educational outcomes of black graduate students?

2. In what ways does race impact mentoring relationships of black graduate students?

Significance of the Research

The significance of this research to the discipline of African American studies is that through effective mentoring, more scholars can be produced to continue the discipline. If the pipeline is indeed empty and there are no black scholars being produced, then hopefully through effective mentoring this trend can be reversed. In recent years, black studies has declined in universities across the United States. Whether this is due to the decline in demand or whether it is believed that black studies is no longer needed is irrelevant. As long as there are blacks in America, black studies programs are needed and as long as black Studies are needed, scholars are needed to teach the discipline. However, scholars are not born. Scholars are made. They are made through teaching and learning.

CHAPTER 2: LITERATURE REVIEW

In her article, "Striving Toward Effective Retention: The Effect of Race on Mentoring African American Students," Wynetta Lee states, "The majority of African American students pursue postsecondary education at predominantly White institutions,[1] and these students have among the lowest completion rates across institutional types."[2]Although other factors may be considered, such as the role community plays in black attrition among graduate students at PWI's and state institutions,[3] it cannot be overlooked that the majority of mentors at PWI's are white and that African-American students are subject to the same cookie-cutter mentoring that is administered to their white counterparts. "The traditional model of mentoring ignores differences between racial and ethnic groups. All graduate students are treated the same, with little regard for strengths or differences that might be due to race and culture."[4] And since ". . .students' interaction with faculty is essential to student retention. . ."[5] It is crucial that black students are able to identify with the person responsible for nurturing them through their

---

[1] Wynetta Y Lee, "Striving Toward Effective Retention: The Effect of Race on Mentoring African American Students," *Peabody Journal of Education* 74, No. 2, Mentoring Underrepresented Students in Higher Education (1999): 28.
[2] Ibid.
[3] Barbara E. Lovitts, *Leaving the Ivory Tower*, (Maryland: Rowman & Littlefield Publishers, 2001), 103.
[4] Martin N. Davidson and Lynn Foster-Johnson, "Mentoring in the Preparation of Graduate Researchers of Color," *Review of Educational Research* 71, No. 4 (2001): 557.
[5] Lee, Striving Toward Effective Retention, 29.

process. At the same time,

> . . .same-race matches for mentors and protégés pose a problem at predominantly White institutions where there is a paucity of African American faculty to pair with African American students. The African American faculties on these campuses are held to the same productivity expectations as other faculty and cannot humanly be expected to mentor all African American students.[6]

That being said, the problem lies not only with the sparse number of African-American faculty available to mentor, but the number of students they are expected to mentor due to the large student-to-teacher ratio. In fact, ". . .many students of color often do not have mentoring relationships. In one study, one third of the African-American graduate students surveyed reported that they had received no mentoring support or guidance in their programs."[7]

In many cases, not only do black students not have mentoring relationships, they do not even have access to mentors.

> . . .having the opportunity to work with same race professors appeared to be difficult for persons of color. Only 7% of the African-American men and women either agreed or strongly agreed that they had adequate opportunities to work with professors of color women of color respondents were least likely to report having a mentor. Moreover, those who had mentors indicated that their mentors were least likely to be in their own units, thus suggesting that these women had to look elsewhere for the type of support that is traditionally given by senior faculty members in their units or departments.[8]

Mentoring is more than just and informal relationship between teacher and student. Mentors are responsible, on some level, for the overall success of their mentee. "An important aspect of the relationship is the assistance and support provided by the

---

[6] Davidson and Foster-Johnson, Mentoring in the Preparation of Graduate Researchers of Color, 550.
[7] Ibid.
[8] Ibid.

mentor to the protégé. Most often, the mentor helps the protégé to achieve long-term and comprehensive goals, in contrast to a teacher or sponsor who may assist with specific activities or short-term tasks."[9]

Therefore, it is little wonder that African-American students seek out same-race mentors. Black students can conceive of their own success in higher education because their black mentor is proof-positive that it is attainable. Also, they may feel that their success is imminent since it is the responsibility of the African-American faculty to take care of their own. "I say have more black male role models. Because if you have black male role models, you'll look at them and say, 'This person has been in the same situation I have, and look how successful he is.'"[10]

Christine Robinson wrote an article in 1999 chronicling her doctoral journey at Peabody College. Although she had attended predominately white institutions for her undergraduate and master's degrees, she always had access to minority support systems. She did not feel isolated. However, at Peabody, she felt locked out of everything that would serve as a support system for her. Instead of succumbing to what could have easily meant defeat, she took steps to not only find what she needed for herself, but also institute programs for other minority students. Robinson was unsure of the reason for the lack of support. "Was the administration unaware of or insensitive to the issues concerning minority graduate students?"[11] She started by talking to the associate dean

---

[9] Ibid.

[10] Terrell L. Strayhorn and Melvin Cleveland Terrell, *The Evolving Challenges of Black College Students: New Insights for Policy, Practice, and Research* (Virginia: Stylus Publishing, 2010), 149.

[11] Christine Robinson, "Developing a Mentoring Program: A Graduate Student's Reflection of Change," *Peabody Journal of Education* 74, No. 2, Mentoring Underrepresented Students in Higher Education (1999): 124.

about the problem. In turn, the associate dean listened, was understanding, and helped organize a social event for the minority students. Although it was an important first step, Robinson knew that one social event would not solve her problem. The first-year doctoral student was in need of a mentor, not just in the academic sense. Robinson contemplated joining a local church to find the kind of nurturing she was seeking, so it is obvious that what was missing was social as well as spiritual - and possibly emotional.

Robinson persisted, despite the associate dean eventually returning to the faculty and a new associate dean replacing her. In many ways, it was like starting over. What she did learn from the experience, however, is that she was not the only black student who felt isolated:

> . . .interviews with minority graduate students suggested that they had less access to faculty members than their White counterparts, had little to no informal and supportive networks on campus, and had difficulties establishing relationships with faculty members.[12]

So, not only was same-race mentoring not available to African-American students, no mentoring was available. Even access to faculty was scarce. For these reasons, Christine Robinson contemplated many times leaving the program. Fortunately, she persevered but she often worried about being labeled a trouble-maker. It is not uncommon to be labeled a troublemaker when you ask for what is right and what is due you. Compounded by that was Christine's race and gender. Black women historically have often been labeled as having an attitude, starting trouble, and being loud. If black women are loud, it is only because it seems our soft voices fall on deaf ears.

---

[12] Ibid.

What Robinson found throughout her quest for change is that in many cases, those in positions to implement change either didn't know there was a problem, didn't know how to address it, or both. She gave administrators the benefit of the doubt in many cases because, quite frankly, they had never dealt with the problem of lack of mentorship and support for black graduate students. "There was much frustration on my part during the meeting process because I thought that the members of the team were more knowledgeable, experienced, and insightful about what to do and would take over and implement the ideas we discussed."[13]

After many meetings, proposals, studies, and interviews, change did occur. A light bulb went off for Christine and she realized that one simple thing could address all of the issues raised by her study:

> I suggested that the group focus its efforts on mentoring. It seemed to be the one thing that could solve many issues raised in the study. Mentoring would address recruitment because it could be used as a tool to attract students to the school and because it offered support services to students on campus. Mentoring would also offer networking with faculty members to students who indicated that they were not given opportunities for professional development in their department.[14]

Christine was able to convince faculty and administrators to test the mentoring idea and after initial success, it was implemented. Although she acknowledges that "Findings from previous studies indicated that matches were more successful if mentors and mentees were of the same race or sex,"[15] successful mentor-mentee relationships were formed between faculty and students of different races. Christine Robinson's article is important for a number of reasons, but for the purpose of this thesis it shows how

---

[13] Ibid., 126.
[14] Ibid.
[15] Ibid., 131.

important mentor relationships are for the educational outcomes of African-American students.

While much emphasis is placed on effective mentoring on education outcomes, Jean Rhodes concedes that ". . .very little is known about the underlying processes by which mentor relationships affect academic outcomes."[16] That is not to say that they do not affect the outcomes, just that the way mentoring relationships affect the outcomes is not known. For example, does having a mentor who believes in a student make that student want to succeed? If so, does having a supportive family work just as well as having an effective mentor at school?

Michael Herndon and Joan Hirt look at same-race mentoring from the family angle. They studied the familial relationships of black college students and mentorship within the family.

> . . .many black students seek support from resources beyond those provided by the campus community, particularly from families. Black students at predominately White institutions rely on support from family members more so than White students at predominately White campuses. . . Therefore, frequent contact with family members is beneficial for black students attending majority institutions.[17]

Herndon's and Hirt's research is important because it charges us to look beyond the university for the mentoring support that keeps students motivated and encouraged. The authors note that ". . .black student retention is related to the support that students receive from family members"[18] and that black families also typically are grounded in

---

[16] Jean E. Rhodes, Jean B. Grossman and Nancy L. Resch *Child Development* 71, No. 6 (2000): 1662
[17] Michael K. Herndon and Joan B. Hirt, "Black Students and Their Families: What Leads to Success in College," *Journal of Black Studies* 34, No. 4 (2004): 491.
[18] Ibid., 493.

religion and therefore have a good emotional and spiritual support system. Black students

can get most of the mentoring they need by starting at home. From supportive parents to

older siblings setting an example, a black student can go to his family for advice,

encouragement and, quite frankly, love. While not all black students have access to a

supportive family, many times coming from broken families, if the outlet is available to

them, they can start there. Black families are a great resource for same-race mentoring

and already in tune to the student's needs.

Herndon and Hirt concluded that familial influence was extremely important in

educational outcomes for black students, undergraduate and graduate. The theme of

mentoring emerged more in graduate students than in undergraduate students and also

included multi-level mentoring where the mentee might also serve as a mentor to

someone in precollege or early college years.

The lack of adequate mentoring is not limited to graduate students of color, but

extends to those who reach the doctoral level. *The Journal of Blacks in Higher Education*

reported that ". . .new African-American Ph.D.s in psychology have had no or inefficient

mentoring." Additionally, Christine Stanley wrote in 2005 that ". . .majority faculty are

reluctant to mentor new faculty of color."[19]

> The black women and other women of color participants in this study indicated
> that they had employed creative strategies to find and develop mentorship
> opportunities outside their own academic units, thereby creating communities of
> resistance. According to one such respondent, a woman of color named Dolores: I
> wasn't aware there was a formal mechanism [of mentorship at the University]. It
> might have been created or put into place since September 1989, but I would say
> that I've been pretty much mentorless my whole way through . . . [T]o survive in
> [my unit], you need to have a fairly strong backbone and . . . fairly strong [sense

[19] Christine A. Stanley and Yvonna S. Lincoln. "Cross-race faculty mentoring", *Change* 37, no. 2 (2005): 46.

of] self-confidence . . . and [be] able to direct and create a sustained research program because . . .help is certainly not going to arrive at your doorstep. You're going to have to go out and seek it. And for the most part, everybody's in it for themselves, so the amount of help that you might get might be advice, but nobody is actually going to give you money. You have to, you know, get in and duke it out.[20]

Authors Gloria D. Thomas and Carol Hollenshead describe mentoring as a coping strategy for women of color, specifically black women, in the academy. They quote Bell Hooks, "I am located in the margin. I make a definite distinction between that marginality which is imposed by oppressive structures and that marginality one chooses as site of resistance-as location of radical openness and possibility"[21] and insist that their marginalized position should not be used to deprive them of the benefits of being in academe. Thomas' and Hollenshead's research is vital for this thesis because it provides a clear reasoning for the lack of minority mentoring available to black students. The authors explain that black faculty, who are already scarce and marginalized, are encouraged to limit their service work and contact with students at all costs, especially if they are not tenured (which is more often than not). It is not that black faculty do not have the time or inclination to mentor black students, it is that they are strongly advised against it. This notion further illustrates the marginal position of black faculty, who can be manipulated and disposed of at will. The ripple effect is that black students end up leaving a university where they feel isolated and neglected. They are counted in the statistics of blacks who drop out of college, further fueling the stereotype that blacks are not cut out for academics and would fare much better in the menial workforce.

---

[20] Gloria Thomas and Carol Hollenshead. "Black Women in the Academy: Challenges and Opportunities," *The Journal of Negro Education* 70, No. 3, (2001): 173.
[21] Ibid.

Thomas' and Hollenshead's research concludes with the idea of becoming creative in negotiating one's space in academe. They advocate seeking out mentors wherever one can find them. They insist that age, interest, and even race are not as important as having the relationship in place. However, given the emphasis they place on the degraded positions of blacks in the academy and the need for mentors for black students and junior faculty, it can be inferred that those relationships would be more fulfilling when fostered by same-race mentors.

> Mentors served as an "insurance policy" against isolation and as a source of motivation and information regarding the pursuit of an administrative position (p. 87). Those women who had the benefit of a role model found the experience so valuable that they tended to become mentors for other women in order to pass along the positive experience.[22]

In conclusion, most scholars agree that a nurturing mentor relationship is more important than having a same-race mentor. However, research does support the notion that the more common the experiences between mentor and mentee, the more nurturing the relationship. So, it is not a stretch to say that African-American mentors are more nurturing to African American students than White students and vice-versa. Edelman puts it this way:

> Many ask today whether black children and youth can benefit from white role models and mentors. Of course they can. While children certainly need mentors with whom they can identify personally from common experiences of race, gender, culture, and economic circumstance, they also need to be shown and taught that human values and caring know no racial or gender boundaries: that all people have something to teach and learn; that race and class need not prevent

---

[22] Kim Allen and Steve Jacobson and Kofi Lomotey. "African American Women in Educational Administration: The Importance of Mentors and Sponsors," *The Journal of Negro Education* 64, No. 4 (1995): 412.

sharing and helping; and that every person is our neighbor and every child our charge.[23]

This research explores the dynamics of mentoring and outcomes. Its focus is on blacks and mentoring relationships in Predominantly White Institutions, as well as research universities. The researcher examined types of mentor-mentee relationships and explore whether or not African-American students perform better, overall, in graduate programs where effective mentoring is implemented.

Conceptual Framework

The framework for this thesis is based on Vincent Tinto's Theory of Academic and Social Adjustment. Tinto posited that students must be socially adjusted in order to be academically adjusted. He attributes attrition to the lack of social adjustment. Utilizing this framework, this thesis explores how mentoring relationships affect graduate student retention and by what means does effective mentoring lead to completion of programs of study. The core concepts of Tinto's theory are pre-entry attributes, goals/commitments, institutional experiences, integration, and outcomes. Pre-entry attributes deals with things a student's readiness for the program. In this case, graduate programs. So, one aspect of pre-entry that was looked at is what type of undergraduate experience did the student have? For example did the student attend an HBCU, PWI or neither? Also, did they attend a large or small college or university? Did they receive a personalized experience or were they just a number?

---

[23] Marian Wright Edelman, *Lanterns: Memoirs of Mentors* (New York: HarperCollins Publishers, 2000), 123.

Goals and commitments deals with what the student is looking to gain from the graduate experience. If there are no clearly-defined goals in place, students are less likely to persist because there is nothing to lose. Institutional experiences is an important theme in this thesis because it deals with things that constructively help or hinder the success of the graduate student. Integration is the core theme of the framework for this thesis because the thesis contends that lack of integration is the major cause of student attrition.

Methodology

The proposed methodology for conducting research is to survey members of the National Black Graduate Student Association. This population represents black graduate students from around the United States. A sample from this group can produce reliable results. Students were asked a range of questions, starting with demographics like what kind of undergraduate institution they attended. They were asked about their mentoring relationships, both formal and informal. If they left their program, they were asked about the reasons they left prior to completion. They also answered questions about their post-program experience. For example, they answered questions about whether they have found employment in their trained field and how satisfied they are about their overall experience. Findings are reported in the Results chapter of the thesis. The results were analyzed to determine if research questions were answered and if the thesis statement was supported by findings.

Study Site and Sample

All active members of the National Black Graduate Student Association were eligible to participate in the study. Questionnaires were administered to those who choose to participate. Since this association is a national representation of black graduate students, a sample of this group produced reliable results.

Limitations

One limitation of this study is attrition by discipline. Blacks account more than half of all graduate students in humanities and social sciences. Incidentally, social sciences have higher attrition rates than other disciplines.

CHAPTER 3: HISTORICAL CHAPTER

History of Mentoring

Historically, a mentor was someone entrusted to care for a student while imparting wisdom. In *The Odyssey*, Mentor was the trusted educator who cared for Telemachus, the son of Odysseus. Mentor was the child's teacher, guide and wise counsel. While the term mentor may have come from Homer's Greek mythology, the actual concept of mentor is much older. In Africa, the notion "It take a village to raise a child" is rooted in the idea of mentoring. In Africa, a series of rituals known as Rites of Passage are used by society to facilitate the transition from childhood to adulthood. There is no period of uncertainty in the African Rites of Passage, as the rituals, once completed, clearly define one as an adult.

Like American students who go off to college and come back adults, African children complete the passage in three stages: separation, transformation, and reincorporation. The children are initially separated from their childhood roles. They are then given a series of rigors to pass, signaling their preparedness for adulthood. Once they have successfully completed their tasks, they are reinstalled into the community as adults. This stage is important because it sends a message to the community that this person shall not be looked upon as inferior, but rather as an equal adult member of the community – with all the rights and responsibilities. When we compare this process to the college student, the completion phase would be the equivalent of completing their studies and returning to their community to work or teach. However, the concept of African Rites of Passage to do not translate linearly in Western constructs. First of all, Western societies stress competition over community. Community is highly-valued in African society and each member has a specified task. Secondly individualism is stressed in most Western cultures. The opposite is true for most African societies. Individuals are revered collectively. Therefore, competition, at least as defined in Western constructs, is eliminated because everyone's role is different and contributes to the whole.

> The educational systems in different kinds of societies in the world have been, and are, very different in organization and content. They are different because societies providing the education are different and because education, whether it be formal or informal, has a purpose. membership of the society and their active participation in its maintenance or development.[1]

Formal mentoring programs in the United States are just over 100 years old; the first being developed just shortly after the implementation of juvenile court systems. It is not coincidence that for about as long as there has been a recognized need for juvenile justice, there has been a need for juvenile intervention. The Big Brothers program was started a few short years after the start of the 20th century and was started out of one man's desire to see a young man succeed in life. Since that time, mentoring has been recognized nationally as important to the future of America's youth. Several presidents and first ladies have acknowledged not only the need, but also the benefits of mentoring. The month of January was designated as National Mentoring Month in 2002.

---

[1] Julius Nyerere. *Education for Self-Reliance* (Government Printer, 1970), 268.

History of Blacks in Higher Education

Although free blacks in America have had access to education for about as long as whites have, the majority of blacks in the United States did not attend schools until the end of slavery. In the 1860's, schools began to sprout up to educate newly-freed blacks. These schools would later become colleges and universities, some Historically black and some state schools. Many were started by free blacks and others by philanthropic whites and abolitionist organizations. Although schools were available, they were not conducive to a proper learning environment. Many black schools had to "make do" with what they had, which was usually leftovers from white schools. However, the lack of decent materials did not stop the process. blacks were learning at accelerated pace and graduating scholars upon scholars. These blacks became leaders in the communities and before long they were holding elected offices throughout the United States. This trend was abruptly halted with the end of the Reconstruction Period in the United States and the introduction of Jim Crow laws.[2]

With the introduction of Jim Crow, it may have seemed that black progress had stopped. However, it terms of education, this was not the case. Blacks continued to attend colleges and universities and earn degrees.[3] However, what they were able to do with those degrees had changed. For most blacks, teaching was the only job an educated black person could get. So, that is what they did. Black teachers taught black students who, in turn, became black teachers. However, the role of teacher encompassed more than just educating the mind of young pupils. Black teachers were surrogate mothers,

---

[2] Harry Morgan. *Historical perspectives on the education of black children* (Connecticut: Spraeger, 1995).
[3] Ibid.

disciplinarians, and social workers to their students. In keeping with the African tradition of the entire village raising the child, teachers were mentors who encouraged their students and offered guidance. Since teaching and mentoring went hand in hand in black schools, it may have appeared that the two were synonymous. After school desegregation, black students began to attend white schools with white teachers.[4] While they may have been receiving the education, they were not getting the nurturing they got in black schools. In black schools, teachers were a part of the black community. So, a teacher could be the mother, the aunt, or even the big sister of students in her class. White teachers were not burdened with the sense of community and obligation to the black students, so all the students received were their lessons. Students that once felt part of a community, a whole, were now being encouraged to compete and to be individualist in their goals and expectations. Many of those who struggled with the new concept were labeled as learning disabled. Those who may have acted out of protest where branded as behaviorally challenged.

This may account for why so many black children were placed in special education. Special education, along with honors and gifted programs, helped resegregate students within the classrooms and schools. Since the landmark Brown case in 1954, black students have been disproportionately placed in special education and behavioral education, while white students have been disproportionately represented in honors and gifted programs.

---

[4] Ibid.

When asked to pinpoint the decline in African American progress in America, many scholars refer to school desegregation.[5] In the process of struggling to attain equality and access to resources, something was lost. In essence, community was traded for a set of new books. Since the mid 1880's most northern communities had public schools in place for blacks. By most standards, these schools were not sub-par and were not established begrudgingly. They were established without legislation. However, with legal obligation to desegregate schools came the backlash and subsequent discrimination. "Blacks in northern cities were now being faced with discrimination in public schools essentially organized by whites."[6]

In conclusion, it is important to note that, as Carter G. Woodson pointed out in *The Education of the Negro Prior to 1861*, education was and is a function of the political climate at any given time. At no time in history, have influential whites been for or against the education of blacks for any humane reason, save the Quakers. African schools have been available since the inception of African slavery, especially before enslavement became a life-condition, where one could not hope for eventual manumission and where offspring were bound by the same terms. Education is at the heart of the culture and as the culture vacillates, so does its position on education. In Mississippi, for example there were no public schools available for blacks *or* whites prior to the Civil War. This fact is an indication of the culture of a state that probably saw no utility in educating a people who were most likely condemned to a life of agriculture. Wealthy whites attended private schools while poor whites worked alongside slaves. In many cases, their condition was

---

[5] Ibid.
[6] Ibid.

no better than a slave's condition – and sometimes worse. The basic needs of slaves were provided for, while whites were responsible for their own meals, clothing, and shelter. After the Civil War, those poor whites became the Night Riders who sought to eliminate competition for the meager jobs that would be available after the country was ravaged by war. Fortunately, public schools were mandated and access to education gave the appearance of propriety and the hope for equality for the next generation, both black and white.

Black Attrition

In furthering the discussion of black student attrition, it cannot be overlooked that lack of mentoring is not the only reasons graduate students leave their enrolled programs. In talking to recruiters who specialize in procuring diverse students, one of the main reasons black students leave graduate school is because they are homesick.[7] In most cases, the homesickness is exacerbated by the lack of familiarity with the new surroundings, especially if their program is in a new city or state. Isolation becomes a key theme when it appears to the student that everyone around them seems to be connected in some way. On PWI campuses, another black face may be few and far in between. Suddenly, the promise of success is not as appealing as having a support system. One recruiter stated that black graduate students are exponentially more likely to travel great distances on the weekends or on breaks than their white counterparts. This undoubtedly creates readjustment anxiety upon return and often the student may not have done any

---

[7] Michael K. Herndon and Joan B. Hirt. *Black Students and Their Families: What leads to success in college. Journal of black Studies 34, no. 4 (March 2004): 489-513.*

work while away, but rather spent time catching up or just enjoying family and friends. So, when papers become due and assigned reading has not occurred, the black student may receive poor grades or get behind in their studies. They may also be reprimanded or chastised, leading to further alienation. In the end, many decide that they would rather have a happy social life than an unhappy academic one.

Just when the black graduate student has gotten settled in socially and adjusted academically, tragedy strikes. Grandma is sick and the student needs to go and "see about" her. Although there are other family members who can and will assist, grandma raised the student and there is an unspoken obligation to go. Even in situations where the student can literally do nothing to help the situation, the canons of the African American family dictate that one must go to see about the ailing member.

Another reason black graduate students leave their programs is money – or lack thereof.[8] While many PhD programs are fully-funded and even include a stipend, many students cannot live off the meager stipend, which is often less than one-third of the average salary they would earn if they entered the workforce with their master's degree. Many black graduate students enter PhD programs from the workforce, not from college, so they have to adjust their life to that of a student. They may have a mortgage, a car payment, and credit card payments to meet. With a PhD at least 5 years away, they cannot always make the adjustment and entice their families to sacrifice during those years. Some take out student loans for living expenses, in addition to their stipend, just to make ends meet. Also, while most programs discourage this practice, some take part-time or full-time jobs. Graduate students receiving stipends are expected to work, in some

---

[8] Ibid.

capacity, at the university in relation to their field of study. This is not only understood, but contractually agreed upon. So, when students attempt to juggle their obligatory work assignments, their classwork, their secondary jobs, and their family obligations, something invariably falls through the cracks. At that point, the only thing expendable is their grades. Eventually their poor grades lead to academic warning, probation, and ultimately dismissal from the program. Some programs will, however, try to console the departing student with a terminal Master's degree based on work already completed. But, for the black graduate student who sacrificed everything to be there, it is a small consolation prize.

While many black graduate students leave school for failure to adjust to their new environment for various reasons, there are cases where the student was never truly prepared to succeed in the program from the beginning. In recent years, the SAT standardized test has been overhaul, largely because of the claims of cultural bias.[9] It is believed that black students performed poorly on the tests because the questions were designed to cater to white culture. It is not that black students were not as smart as whites, it is just that they were not taught the things that the SAT tested. This is great news for test-takers, but does nothing for black graduate students at PWI. They enter a world that was not designed with them in mind, and therefore find it difficult to flourish. What may have been an acceptable paper at their undergraduate institution might be considered an utter failure at their PWI. What's more, their white professor may assume that laziness and a lack of effort contributed more to their unacceptable work than lack of

---

[9] Terrell L.Strayhorn and M. Terrell. The Evolving Challenges of Black College Students. Virginia: Stylus Publishing, 2010.

knowledge or preparation. As a result, the black graduate student receives poor grades that eventually lead to attrition, rather than preparation. Giving poor grades instead of further instruction may be considered a form of poor treatment, but there are others that eventually lead to a black student leaving their program. Discrimination is a form of poor treatment that can range from subtle to overt. Subtle forms may be things like assuming something about the person because they are black. More overt discrimination can be something like asking the student if they wouldn't be happier at an HBCU. Poor treatment can be disseminated by the university, its representatives, or its students. White students may view their black counterparts as freeloaders who got where they are because of affirmative action or some other equalization program. They may not take their black colleagues seriously, refusing to work with them. This can lead to further isolation. And as Tinto posits, isolation leads to student attrition. Johnson and Huwe discuss in their book, *Getting Mentored in Graduate School*,[10] four common problems in cross-cultural mentorships. Among the problems is mistrust. That mistrust can stem from believing that the other person in the relationship does not deserve to be there and they got where they are because of quotas or a system designed to promote the majority race, regardless of qualifications. Cross-culture mentor relationships are often encumbered from the start by this mistrust. To further complicate the process, Johnson and Huwe discuss the struggle for power a common problem in these relationships.

It is not uncommon for the majority race to act paternalistically towards blacks, thinking that they know what is best based on historical authoritarian roles over them – however ill-gotten. It is not a stretch to say that the lasting effects of slavery can hinder

---

[10] Brad Johnson and Jennifer Huwe. *Getting Mentored in Graduate School.* 2003.

something so rudimentary as a mentor relationship when the structure of that relationship resembles that of the master and his slave. If the white mentor acts in an omnipotent and unyielding manner towards his minority protégé, he alienates the student before any instruction or direction can be given. Johnson and Huwe refer to this difference in interpersonal style as the third common problem in cross-cultural mentoring relationships.[11] The fourth and final common problem stems from the protégé's difficulty asking for help. Johnson and Huwe posit that most minority students who have reached graduate-level programs have done so on their own merit and as a result of their own hard work.[12] So, when placed in a relationship where they find themselves on the end where help is solicited, it can be construed as weakness or even failure.

While many of these problems exist in the minds of the mentor and protégé and can often be solved with open and frank communication, they cannot be discounted as invalid. The research strongly suggests that having same-race mentors improves educational outcomes of graduate students. It does not show that cross-cultural mentor relationships hinder outcomes. Conversely, the research shows that simply having a mentor improves retention and persistence. Having same-race mentors improves completion rates among African-American students. However, because of gross underrepresentation of minority faculty at most American universities, this kind of mentoring relationship is not always available.

---

[11] Ibid.
[12] Ibid.

Mentoring as Part of the Curriculum

At universities like University of Michigan and Georgia State University where mentoring is part of the graduate curriculum and not just an afterthought or option, record numbers of minority PhD are produced on a yearly basis. It is further evidence of the correlation between mentoring and persistence, especially among minorities. At many universities, internships are the only form of mentoring that are a part of the curriculum. When we consider the fact that not every student will have the opportunity to participate in an internship or that internships are only for a semester, it is of little benefit. The fact that the U.S. has the worst school-to-work transition of any industrialized nation in the world is proof that what is being taught in the classroom is not translating to meaningful execution of skills obtained. Mentoring is the social catalyst that can ease the transition and, as Vincent Tinto suggests, lead to persistence.[13]

When Mentoring Does Not Work

While a preponderance of the evidence supports the notion that mentoring works and is likely the most effective tool in promoting persistence, there is evidence that in some cases mentoring does not work. Catherine A. Hansman points out in *Ethical Issues in Mentoring Adults in Higher Education* ethical issues to consider when undertaking the role of mentor.[14] Hansman maintains that, by the nature of the relationship, mentors have the power to help or harm the people they mentor. She concludes that this is a source of

---

[13] Vincent Tinto. *Leaving College: Rethinking the Causes and Cures of Student Attrition.* Chicago: University Of Chicago Press, 1994.

[14] Katherine Hansman. *Ethical Issues in Mentoring Adults in Higher Education. New Directions in Adult Continuing Education.* 123. Fall 2009.

ethical issues.[15] For example, Hansman was strongly opposed to ideology in one of her students' dissertations. She notified the student that she would not continue as co-chair if the students did not change certain statements. The student begrudgingly made the changes and eventually graduated. However, the student felt that her progress was hindered as a result of the delays.

Hansman insists it was the students' inability to back up her claims with proper research that hindered her progress.[16] Nonetheless, Hansman's disagreement with the unsubstantiated claims negatively impacted the student's completion.[17] In another instance, Hansman described being overly sympathetic to a student's personal situation and spending less time focusing on the goals of the student. Hansman realized that she was doing a disservice to the student by acting more like a sounding board than a mentor. She soon began to curb the personal conversations and redirect the student to her academic goals. Only then was the student able to refocus and work towards completion of her dissertation.

Hansman describes several similar scenarios in her book chapter in which mentoring can be cumbersome, if not problematic. Hansman's role as a mentor was secondary to her job as an educator. However, she reflects in each scenario ways in which she could have improved her interaction with her protégé. She also maintains that she acted in good faith and overall completion rates were positive for students she mentored. She notes that many of those students later reported overall satisfaction with

---

[15] Ibid.
[16] Ibid.
[17] Ibid.

their experience. Therefore, even in cases where mentoring can have adverse effects in the short term, long term benefits can still be achieved.

CHAPTER 4: RESULTS

In a survey of 105 current and former black graduate students across the United States, 84.4% of the respondents cited "sheer will and determination" as a factor which contributed to their graduate school success. The survey was administered through various black Graduate Student Associations, with 98.8% of the respondents having been enrolled in a graduate program of study within the last ten years. The survey was used to determine what factors contribute to completion of programs among black graduate students.

The second most contributing factor to black graduate student success was peer support. Just over 72% of respondents considered the support of their peers as a factor in their success. Additionally, 66.2% believed that faculty support contributed to their success, with family close behind at 64.9%. Surprisingly, just over half (53.2%) cited "spirituality" as a factor to their success. This is surprising considering the influence of the church in African American lives. Faith has long been associated with success among African Americans. However, the results of this survey suggest that black graduate students do not rely on their spirituality as much as they rely on themselves and their peers. Also, 84.4% of respondents believed it was due to their own will and determination that they succeeded in their program of study.

Other results of the survey reveal that 6.5% of respondents cited "other" factors that included, specifically mentor support (select faculty relationships), counseling, Jesus, financial support by employer, and all of the above. While most of these "other" responses could have fit into one of the specific categories, the write-in responses indicate the importance of these factors as relates to the individuals who cited them.

With the attrition rate of black graduate students at 50% nationally, compared to just 25% for whites, this information is important for universities in their retention efforts. Twice as many black graduate students are leaving their programs of study, and this kind of disparity must not go unexamined if proportionate numbers of black scholars are to be produced.

It is important to note that all of the respondents either completed their program or are currently enrolled. None of the respondents left their program without completing. 84.5% of the respondents attended a Predominately White Institution (PWI) for their graduate program and 67.5% attended a PWI as an undergraduate. 63.8% of respondents had a mentor in graduate school. 31.5% believed that race was a factor in the pairing of them with their mentor. Other results show that of the 62% of respondents who had a mentor, 51% of them said their mentor was a different race. This revelation indicates further that race is not a significant factor in mentoring relationships that foster a culture of completion. This notion is further supported by the 57% who stated outright that race was not a factor in their pairing with a mentor.

Of the more than 100 respondents, 64% consider their graduate school experience a success and 72% said their overall experience was satisfactory. These findings are consistent with the thesis statement that black graduate students who participate in mentoring relationships consider their overall experience a success. Additionally, 43% had GPAs of 3.8-4.0. This is also consistent with the thesis statement that black graduate students who participate in mentoring relationships have higher overall GPAs than their non-mentored counterparts. The 52% of respondents who participated in organizations in graduate school likely experienced some form of peer mentoring by participating in such organizations. Finally, the 64% of respondents who did not have family members in the city where they attended graduate school likely found support in their peers, the second most reported contributing factor in graduate school success.

Ellemers tied the top two contributing factors to success in this way: black graduate students with high salience were more likely to display a "sticking together" reaction when they perceived their existence to be threatened. So, the sheer will and determination they possessed individually translated to support for their peers as well. Their own-group conformity dictated that not only was *one* going to make it (complete the program), they were *all* going to make it – as one unit.[1]

As stated in the introduction, the purpose of this thesis is to explore mentor relationships to determine what factors impact black students' completion of graduate programs of study. Mentor relationships between faculty and students appeared to be significant, based on existing literature. However, the results of the survey revealed that mentors that had the most significant impact on completion were informal peer mentors.

---

[1] Naimi Ellemers, R.ussell Spears, and Bertjan Doosje, "Sticking together or falling apart: Ingroup identification as a psychological determinant of group commitment versus individual mobility." *Journal of Personality and Social Psychology* 72, no. 3, (1997): 617-626.

black graduate students depend on themselves and their peers more than their faculty, families, or even spiritual leaders.

This research set out to examine the ways in which mentoring impacts black graduate students decision to complete their programs of study and what factors ultimately cause some to leave their programs of study without completing. The outcome of these inquires suggest that neither race, age, nor gender of faculty mentors was a significant factor in the pairing of mentors and mentees. Further, the results of the survey show that having a faculty mentor or not did not impact students decisions to leave their programs of study. Factors that impacted students' decision to leave their program were unrelated to whether or not they had a faculty mentor.

Since the existing literature suggested that same-race mentoring was a significant factor in educational outcomes of black graduate students, this paper set out to explore the need for more black faculty at PWI's and in what ways mentoring relationships can benefit black graduate students. An interesting outcome of this survey is that race was a non-factor in completion of programs by black graduate students. Research questions that were answered as a result of the survey:

1. In what ways does mentoring affect performance and educational outcomes of black graduate students? Performance is measured in terms of grades, percentage of program completion, length of time to complete program, and overall attitude about their graduate experience.

Based on the results of the survey, the answer appears to be that mentoring positively affects educational outcomes of black graduate students. 62% of the respondents had mentors, 43% had GPA above 3.8, less than 1% of the respondents did not complete their program of study, 30% finished in less than 3 years, and 62% felt their experience was a success.

2. In what ways does race impact mentoring relationships of black graduate students?

Race of mentors appears to be insignificant when it comes to impact of black graduate students. 87% of the respondents attended PWI, and 51% had different race mentors, yet 99% completed their program of study or are still enrolled. Therefore, it appears that the race of the mentor does not have an impact on completion for black graduate students. This is contrary to the existing literature, which suggests that it does.

3. What is the significance of the research?

The significance of this research to the discipline of African American studies is that through effective mentoring, more scholars can be produced to continue the discipline. Just as the existing literature suggests, mentoring is significant to educational outcomes. However, the race of the mentor is irrelevant to the success of the black graduate student. Further, mentoring by faculty is less important than peer mentoring, where an astonishing 72.7% attribute their success to their peers.

4. What is the relationship between mentoring and outcomes?

This research will explore the dynamics of mentoring and outcomes. As the below tables show, there is a positive correlation between students who have mentors and their educational outcomes.

Limitations

As with any research, this thesis has some limitations. For one, some students may be unwilling to admit that they did not complete their program of study. They may have reported "currently enrolled", even if they are not enrolled in the *current* semester. Another limitation is that students who did not complete their program may not be active in graduate student association and therefore may not have completed the survey. Finally, students who are active members of student associations are more likely to be currently enrolled. Alumni associations, by definition, are just that – for alum. They may not reflect currently enrolled students.

CHAPTER 5: CONCLUSIONS

In conclusion, while initially thought to be significant, it appears that black graduate students do not necessarily believe that mentor and faculty support is an important factor in their success. Of those students with mentors, over half had mentors of different race. So, it appears that same-race mentoring is not important for completion of their program, graduate school success, or an overall satisfactory experience.

More than 87% of the respondents attended a Predominantly White Institution. This is significant when we consider that none of the respondents left their program without completion, and 57% felt that race was not a factor in the pairing of mentors and mentees.

While the existing literature suggests that black graduate students lack same-race mentoring and assimilation into graduate programs of study, the results of this research conclude that attending Predominantly White Institutions and having different-race mentoring relationships is not a recipe for attrition among African American students. The results show that black graduate students have overwhelming taken responsibility for their own success and each other's success. Another significant outcome of the research is that 72.7% of respondents considered the support of their peers as a factor in their success. This result is consistent with Tinto's theory of social adjustment. Since they considered their peers as factors in their successful outcome of completion, it can be inferred that they were socially adjusted among their peers. Just over 50% of the students participated in social organizations.

This speaks specifically to social adjustment. Another 17% participated in other organizations, most of which include black graduate support organizations and other groups specific to African American graduate students. This is even more significant than the 50% that participated in social organizations because it implies, if not specifically states that black graduate students are not only cognizant of their unique need, but are vigilant in remedying it by participating in groups with others that share their same plight. It is important to note, though, that graduate student organizations are required to have a faculty sponsor. So, it is possible that while participating in student organizations, graduate students are receiving healthy, informal interaction with faculty that encourages them in ways it cannot occur in the classroom. Johnson and Nelson found that mutual support and comprehensive relationships, in both formal and informal settings, were the two most important factors that contribute to successful mentoring of graduate students.[1]

The survey revealed that 64% of black graduate students do not have family members in the city where they attend their program. Therefore, social adjustment is even more important since family is not immediately available for support. Based on the results, it appears that black graduate students "psyche" themselves up to persist in their programs through sheer will and determination first, then turn to their peers for the rest of the support they need. What are they getting from their peers that they cannot get from their faculty mentor? Often, faculty are the *problem*. Black graduate students need a sounding board and they find it in their peers. They may talk to their peers about the faculty members with whom they are having problems. "My faculty mentor is

---

[1] William Brad Johnson and Neal Nelson. "Mentor-protégé' relationships in graduate training: Some ethical concerns." *Ethics & Behavior* 9, no. 3 (1999): 189–210.

unorganized", "My professor doesn't like me", or "My professor is too hard on me." They can say these things to their black graduate student peers. They can't say these things to their faculty, who ultimately control their grades, and in turn, their fate. Black graduate students can persist when they know they are not the only ones experiencing the problems they are facing. When they talk to their peers, they realize they are not the only ones dealing with certain problems. They realize that other students are suffering the same difficulties. So, they can persist because they know they are not alone. They know that the problem is not unique to them. While most do thrive off sheer will and determination, many thrive off of the support they get from their peers. In conclusion, while mentoring is an important part of black graduate student success, it does not always come from the faculty mentor, but often the informal peer mentor.

While faculty support, i.e. mentoring, appears to be important, it does not appear to be the driving force behind persistence in black graduate students, despite the fact that graduate students "consider their relations with faculty members to be one of the most important factors in determining the quality of their educational experience."[2]

---

[2] Debra S. Schroeder and Clifford R. Mynatt. "Female graduate students' perceptions of their interactions with male and female major professors." *The Journal of Higher Education* 64, *(1993)*: 555–573.

APPENDIX A

Consent for Participation in Interview Research

I volunteer to participate in a research project conducted by Nicole Sullivan from Clark Atlanta University. I understand that the project is designed to gather information about mentors and mentees, and my experience as a graduate student. I will be one of approximately 25 people who will either respond to a questionnaire, be interviewed about my graduate school experience, or both.

My participation in this project is voluntary. I understand that I will not be paid for my participation. I may withdraw and discontinue participation at any time without penalty. If I decline to participate or withdraw from the study, that information will not be disclosed.

I understand that I have the right to decline to answer any questions or to end the interview.

Participation involves being interviewed by Nicole Sullivan of Clark Atlanta University. The questionnaire is approximately 25 questions and may take approximately one hour to complete. I understand that the interview, if I am selected, will last approximately 30-45 minutes. I understand that my responses may be recorded.

I understand that the researcher will not identify me by name in any reports using information obtained from this interview, and that my anonymity as a participant in this study will remain secure. Subsequent uses of records and data will be subject to standard data use policies, which protect the anonymity of individuals and institutions.

Faculty and administrators from my campus will neither be present at the interview nor have access to raw notes or transcripts. This precaution will prevent my individual comments from having any negative repercussions.

I understand that this research study has been reviewed and approved by the Institutional Review Board (IRB) for Studies Involving Human Subjects.

APPENDIX B

Questionnaire for Black graduate students – Nicole Sullivan

I.   Background questions

1. What type of undergraduate institution did you attend? HBCU, PWI, Research University, Community College, Faith-based institution, other?
2. At what age did you begin your graduate program?
3. Why did you choose this institution?
4. What did you expect to gain from attending this graduate institution?
5. What is your mission?

II.   Questions about your experience in the program

1. What factors contributed to your success (if you feel you are successful)?
2. Did any faculty or students help you?
3. Did you participate in clubs, sororities, fraternities, etc., while working on your undergraduate degree?
4. Describe the most important thing that happened to you while in college:
5. What instructor had the most impact?
6. Did you complete your program? If yes, answer the following question:
7. How many years did it take you to complete your program of study?
8. What is the average length of time to complete your particular program?

9. In the city where you attend(ed) your program of study, do you have family members? Yes or no

III. Questions about your mentor experience

1. If you are currently enrolled in a graduate program of study, do you currently have a mentor? Yes, no, or not currently enrolled
2. If you completed your program, did you have a mentor? Yes, no, or did not complete program
3. If you left the program before completion, did you have a mentor? Yes, no, or I completed my program
4. If you have or had a mentor, was he or she the same race as you? Yes, no, or I did not have a mentor
5. If you had or have a mentor, did you all discuss race at all? Yes, no, or did not have /do not have a mentor
6. How comfortable are you/were you with your mentor? Very comfortable, just comfortable, not so comfortable, or did not have a mentor

IV. Post-program questions

1. What is your overall GPA upon completion of your program?
2. How would you rate your overall graduate experience on a scale of 1 to 5, where 1 is terrible, 2 is tolerable, 3 is fair, 4 is good, and 5 is exceptional?
3. Since completion, have you been offered employment in your field?
4. Are you willing to participate in an interview?
5. Do you know anyone who left the program in which you were/are enrolled? If so, do you know why they left the program? Do you keep in contact? Do you think they would be willing to participate in this study?

CLARK ATLANTA UNIVERSITY
Institutional Review Board
Office of Sponsored Programs

September 28, 2012

Ms. Nicole Sullivan <nicole.sullivan@students.cau.edu>
Dept. of African-American Studies
McPheeters Dennis #6
Clark Atlanta University
Atlanta, GA 30314

RE: Same Race Mentoring and Educational Outcomes.

Principal Investigator(s): Nicole Sullivan

Human Subjects Code Number: HR2012-9-450-1

Dear Ms. Sullivan:

The Human Subjects Committee of the Institutional Review Board (IRB) has reviewed
your protocol and approved of it as exempt in accordance with 45 CFR 46.101(b)(2).

Your Protocol Approval Code is HR2012-9-450-1/A

This permit will expire on September 29, 2013. Thereafter, continued approval is
contingent upon the annual submission of a renewal form to this office.
The CAU IRB acknowledges your timely completion of the CITI IRB Training in Protection
of Human Subjects – "Social and Behavioral Sciences Track". Your certification is valid
for two years.

If you have any questions, please contact Dr. Georgianna Bolden at the Office of
Sponsored Programs (404) 880-6979 or Dr. Paul I. Musey, (404) 880-6829.

Sincerely:

Paul I. Musey, Ph.D.
Chair
IRB: Human Subjects Committee

cc. Office of Sponsored Programs, "Dr. Georgianna Bolden" <gbolden@cau.edu>

BIBLIOGRAPHY

Almost No Blacks in Academic Psychology: Does the Pipeline Defense Hold Water? *The Journal of Blacks in Higher Education* no. 34 (Winter 2001): 48-49.

It's Time to do Better: A Count of Black Students and Faculty at the Nation's 50 Flagship State Universities. *The Journal of Blacks in Higher Education* no. 32 (Summer 2001): 86-92.

Allen, Kim, Steve Jacobson, and Kofi Lomotey. African American Women in Educational Administration: The Importance of Mentors and Sponsors. *The Journal of Negro Education* 64, no. 4 (Autumn 1995): 409-422.

Allen, Walter R., Edgar G. Epps, Elizabeth A. Guillory, Susan A. Suh, and Marguerite Bonous-Hammarth. *The Black Academic: Faculty Status Among African-Americans in U.S. Higher Education. The Journal of Negro Education* 69, no. 1/2, Knocking at Freedom's Door: Race, Equity, and Affirmative Action in U.S. Higher Education: (Winter-Spring 2000): 112-127.

Crawford, Kijana and Danielle Smith. *The We and the Us: Mentoring African-American Women. Journal of Black Studies* 36, no. 1 (September 2005): 52-67.

Dixon-Reeves, Regina. Mentoring as a Precursor to Incorporation: *An Assessment of the Mentoring Experience of Recently Minted Ph.D.s. Journal of Black Studies* 34, no. 1 (September 2003), Race in the Academy: Moving beyond Diversity and toward the Incorporation of Faculty of Color in Predominantly White Colleges and Universities: pp. 12-27.

Davidson, Martin N. and Lynn Foster-Johnson. *Mentoring in the Preparation of Graduate Researchers of Color. Review of Educational Research* 71, no. 4 (Winter 2001): 549-574.

Edelman, Marian Wright. *Spelman college: A Safe Haven for a Young Black Woman. The Journal of Blacks in Higher Education* no. 27 (Spring 2000): 118-123.

Farley, John E. 2002. *Contesting our everyday work lives: The retention of minority and working-class sociology undergraduates. The Sociological Quarterly* 43, no. 1 (Winter 2000): 1-25.

Green, Anna L. and K. Scott. *Journey to the PhD: How to Navigate the Process as African Americans.* Virginia: Stylus Publishing, 2003.

Hansman, Katherine. *Ethical Issues in Mentoring Adults in Higher Education. New Directions in Adult Continuing Education.* 123. Fall 2009.

Herndon, Michael K. and Joan B. Hirt. *Black Students and Their Families: What leads to success in college. Journal of Black Studies* 34, no. 4 (March 2004): 489-513.

Johnson, Brad and Jennifer Huwe. *Getting Mentored in Graduate School.* 2003.

Lee, Wynetta Y. *Striving toward effective retention: The Effect of Race on Mentoring African-American Students. Peabody Journal of Education* 74, no. 2 (Winter-Spring 1999), Mentoring Underrepresented Students in Higher Education: 27-43.

Leon, David J. *Mentoring Minorities in Higher Education: Passing the Torch.* Washington: National Education Association, 1997.

Lovitts, Barbara E. *Leaving the Ivory Tower*. Maryland:Rowman & Littlefield Publishers, 2001.

Moberg, Dennis J., and Manuel Velasquez. *The Ethics of Mentoring. Business Ethics Quarterly* 14.1 (January 2004): pp. 95-122.

Morgan, Harry. *Historical Perspectives on the Education of Black Children.* Connecticut: Spraeger, 1995.

National Center for Education Statistics, http://nces.ed.gov/fastfacts/display.asp?id=72 (accessed July 26, 2012).

Nyerere, Julius. *Education for Self-Reliance*. Government Printer, 1970.

Okawa, Gail Y. Diving for pearls: *Mentoring as Cultural and Activist Practice Among Academics of Color. College Composition and Communication* 53, no. 3 (February 2002): 507-532.

Olson, Carol. *Recruiting and Retaining Minority Graduate Students: A Systems Perspective. The Journal of Negro Education* 57, no. 1(Winter 1988): 31-42.

Omolewa, Michael. *Traditional African Modes of Education: Their Relevance in the Modern World. International Review of Education / Internationale Zeitschrift Für Erziehungswissenschaft / Revue Internationale De l'Education* 53, no. 5/6 (November 2007), Quality Education in Africa: Challenges and Prospects: 593-612.

Paglis, Laura L., Stephen G. Green, and Talya N. Bauert. *Does Adviser Mentoring Add Value? A Longitudinal Study of Mentoring and Doctoral Student Outcomes. Research in Higher Education* 47.4 (June 2006): pp. 451-476.

Rhodes, Jean E., Jean B. Grossman, and Nancy L. Resch. *Agents of Change: Pathways Through Which Mentoring Relationships Influence Adolescents' Academic Adjustment. Child Development* 71, no. 6 (Nov 2000): 1662-1671.

Robinson, Christine. *Developing a Mentoring Program: A Graduate Student's Reflection of Change. Peabody Journal of Education* 74, no. 2 (1999), Mentoring Underrepresented Students in Higher Education: 119-134.

Rubin, Beth C. *Unpacking Detracking: When Progressive Pedagogy Meets Students' Social Worlds. American Educational Research Journal* 40, no. 2 (Summer 2003): 539-573.

Stanley, Christine A. and Yvonna S. Lincoln. *Cross-Race Faculty Mentoring. Change* 37, no. 2 (March-April 2005): 44-50.

Strayhorn, Terrell L. and M. Terrell. *The Evolving Challenges of Black College Students.* Virginia: Stylus Publishing, 2010.

Thomas, Gloria D. and Carol Hollenshead. *Resisting From the Margins: The Coping Strategies of Black Women and Other Women of Color Faculty Members at a Research University. The Journal of Negro Education* 70, no. 3 (Summer 2001), Black Women in the Academy: Challenges and Opportunities: 166-175.

Tillman, Linda C. *Mentoring African-American Faculty in Predominantly White Institutions. Research in Higher Education* 42, no. 3 (June 2001): 295-325.

Tinto, Vincent. *Leaving College: Rethinking the Causes and Cures of Student Attrition.* Chicago: University Of Chicago Press, 1994.

Townsend, Laird. *How Universities Successfully Retain and Graduate Black Students. The Journal of Blacks in Higher Education* no. 4 (Summer 1994): 85-89.

Turabian, Kate L. *A Manual for Writers of Research Papers, Theses, and Dissertations.* Chicago: University of Chicago Press, 2007.

U.S. Department of Education, http://www.ed.gov/ (accessed July 26, 2012).

Warfield-Coppock, Nsenga. *The Rites of Passage Movement: A Resurgence of African-Centered Practices for Socializing African-American Youth. The Journal of Negro Education* 61, no. 4 (Autumn 1992): 471-482.

Wright Edelman, Marian. *Lanterns: Memoirs of Mentors*. New York: HarperCollins Publishers, 2000.

www.ingramcontent.com/pod-product-compliance
Lightning Source LLC
Chambersburg PA
CBHW080904290526
45795CB00007BA/2405